Mount Rushmore

By Karen Latchana Kenney
Illustrated by Judith A. Hunt

Content Consultant:
Richard Jensen, PhD
Author, Scholar, and Historian

magic wagon

visit us at www.abdopublishing.com

Looking Glass Library™ is a trademark and logo of Magic Wagon.

Printed in the United States of America, North Mankato, Minnesota.
092010
012011

 THIS BOOK CONTAINS AT LEAST 10% RECYCLED MATERIALS.

Text by Karen Latchana Kenney
Illustrations by Judith A. Hunt
Edited by Melissa Johnson
Interior layout and design by Becky Daum
Cover design by Becky Daum

Library of Congress Cataloging-in-Publication Data
Kenney, Karen Latchana.
  Mount Rushmore / by Karen Latchana Kenney ; illustrated by Judith A. Hunt.
    p. cm. — (Our nation's pride)
  Includes index.
  ISBN 978-1-61641-153-4
  1. Mount Rushmore National Memorial (S.D.)—Juvenile literature. I. Hunt, Judith A., 1955- ill. II. Title.
  F657.R8K46 2011
  978.3'93—dc22
                          2010014009

Table of Contents

Big Art

In South Dakota, a stony mountain juts into the sky. One side of the mountain is a giant work of art. Large faces look out across the land.

The faces belong to past presidents of the United States. They are George Washington, Thomas Jefferson, Theodore Roosevelt, and Abraham Lincoln. Years ago, the faces were carved into this mountain called Mount Rushmore.

4

Sacred Land

The land in western South Dakota is very special. Beautiful mountains and deep canyons fill the Black Hills. Long before Mount Rushmore was carved, the Lakota people lived here. They believed the land was sacred.

In 1868, the U.S. government promised that the Lakotas could live in the Black Hills forever. But when white settlers found gold there, they took the land from the Lakotas.

A Monument in the Black Hills

In the 1920s, not many people traveled to

South Dakota. Doane Robinson worked for the

state. He needed a way to bring visitors there.

Robinson had an idea. What if there were

a big monument in the Black Hills? It could be

carved into a mountain. Visitors would come to

see it. Not everyone agreed. The Lakotas thought a

monument would destroy the sacred land.

STATE OF SOUTH DAKOTA

DEPARTMENT OF HISTORY

August 29 1934

Mr Gutzon Borglum
Stone Mountain, Georgia

Dear Mr Borglum

In the vicinity of Harney Peak, in the Black Hills of South Dakota are opportunities for heroic sculpture of unusual character. Would it be possible for you to design and supervise a massive sculpture there? The proposal has not passed beyond the mere suggestion, but if it be possible for you to undertake the matter I feel quite sure we could arrange to finance such an enterprise. I should be glad to hear from you at your convenience.

Faithfully,

Doane Robinson, Supt.

The Perfect Mountain

Robinson looked for someone to make the monument. Gutzon Borglum was an artist with big ideas. Robinson wrote to him about his plan for the Black Hills.

Soon after, Borglum visited the area. He had to see what the rock was like. Mount Rushmore was made of the right kind of granite. It had a wall big enough for the sculpture. It was perfect!

Important Men

Borglum wanted the monument to be important to all Americans. Four presidents' faces would be carved. George Washington was the nation's first president. Thomas Jefferson wrote the Declaration of Independence. Abraham Lincoln ended slavery and kept the United States together in the American Civil War. The country grew in power and wealth while Theodore Roosevelt was president.

A Plaster Model

Borglum made a plaster model of the monument. Every feature on the model was measured. Each inch equaled a foot on the mountain. When the models were finished, marks were painted onto the mountain. They showed where to carve. Borglum planned very carefully. It would be difficult to make the real carving look like the model.

14

The Workers

A lot of workers were needed for the big project. Miners knew about working with rock. Powdermen knew how to use dynamite. Mechanics knew how to run the machines that were used.

The workers would need to be brave to walk up and down the face of the mountain. They would hang from the top of the mountain. They would wear special harnesses that Borglum designed.

Carving the Mountain

In 1927, carving on the monument began.

Workers put dynamite into holes in the rock. Then,

they had to get off the mountain. The dynamite

exploded! Big chunks of rock fell everywhere. With

many explosions, the face of each president took

shape on the mountain.

The drillers then took over. They cut down the stone even more. Hanging on to the drills was hard. Each drill weighed about half as much as the person who used it.

Carvers finished up. They worked on a small area at a time. They made small holes in the rock so they could carve details. The holes made the rock look like a honeycomb. Next, the carvers used drills to remove the honeycomb area. Then, they used hammers to smooth the rock.

Finally Finished

In 1930, George Washington's head was finished. Then Thomas Jefferson and Abraham Lincoln were carved. The last head was Theodore Roosevelt. Mount Rushmore was finished in 1941—14 years after work began.

Since then, the monument has needed repairs. The dynamite weakened the rock, and it cracks often. Before the cracks grow, they are filled with a mixture. It keeps out water and protects the rock.

22

The Hall of Records

A special room called the Hall of Records was cut into Mount Rushmore. It was never finished. The room holds a time capsule. Inside it are special plates that are meant to last forever.

Writing on the plates tells about the monument and the four presidents. It also describes the history of the United States. People in the future may one day find the box. It will help them understand our history.

Mount Rushmore Today

Mount Rushmore is more than a carving of four presidents. It is a symbol of the United States. It tells the history of the country and its leaders.

In 2004, an American Indian man became the caretaker of Mount Rushmore for the first time. He added new programs and new museum exhibits. Now, the monument also tells the story of the Lakota and other American Indians who first lived in the Black Hills.

A Visit to Mount Rushmore

You can get to Mount Rushmore National Park by bus or by car. Walk down the Avenue of Flags. Look in a studio to see Borglum's model. See the tools that were used to carve the mountain.

You can also walk on a trail. A ranger can tell you the history of the monument. At night, the park has a show. It ends with lights shining on beautiful Mount Rushmore.

Fun Facts

- How big are the faces on Mount Rushmore? Each head is 60 feet (18 m) tall. That is as tall as a six-story building! Each eye is 11 feet (3 m) wide. Each mouth is 18 feet (5 m) wide. George Washington's nose is 21 feet (6 m) long. The other presidents' noses are 20 feet (6 m) long.

- Thomas Jefferson's head was supposed to be on the right side of George Washington. Workers cut the stone, but it was not strong enough for the sculpture. They blasted away their work. Then they put Jefferson's head on the other side of Washington.

- Borglum wanted the monument to show the presidents down to their waists. The project ran out of money though. So, only the heads of the presidents were completed!

Glossary

carve—to cut and shape rock.

dynamite—a powerful explosive.

granite—a very hard rock used in buildings.

harness—a system of straps and belts that helps keep someone safe.

honeycomb—rows of holes that are arranged in a pattern going up and down and across.

plaster—a mixture of lime, sand, and water that sticks to a surface.

sacred—to have religious meaning for some people.

sculpture—a piece of art that is carved from stone, wood, metal, marble, or clay.

symbol—something that stands for something else.

On the Web

To learn more about Mount Rushmore, visit ABDO Group online at **www.abdopublishing.com**. Web sites about Mount Rushmore are featured on our Book Links page. These links are routinely monitored and updated to provide the most current information available.

Index